The Best T~~ail~~ | ~~7~~
Cook~~~~

Elevate Your Pre-Game Experience with 100
Mouthwatering Recipes and Winning Tips

TRISTAN MATTHEWS

TABLE OF CONTENTS

INTRODUCTION

Welcome to The Best Tailgating Cookbook! This cookbook is your all-in-one guide to mastering the art of tailgating cuisine and turning your pre-game gatherings into unforgettable feasts. Whether you're a seasoned tailgater or a newbie looking to join the excitement, get ready to take your game day experience to a whole new level.

In this cookbook, we've curated a collection of crowd-pleasing recipes that will fuel your spirit and satisfy your taste buds. From classic comfort foods like juicy burgers and finger-licking wings to creative twists on game day favorites, we've got you covered. Prepare to dazzle your fellow fans with mouthwatering dishes that are easy to make, transport, and enjoy in the stadium parking lot.

But this cookbook is not just about recipes. We'll also share winning tips and tricks for setting up the ultimate tailgate party, from essential equipment and organization hacks to game day activities that will keep everyone entertained. Whether you're tailgating at a football game, a concert, or any other event, our goal is to make your pre-game experience memorable, delicious, and full of camaraderie.

Get ready to create a winning spread that will make you

the MVP of every tailgate party. Let the games begin!

1. Grilled Chicken Wings

Ingredients:
- 2 lbs chicken wings
- 1/2 cup BBQ sauce
- 1/4 cup honey
- 1/4 cup soy sauce
- 2 garlic cloves, minced
- 1 tsp ground ginger
- Salt and pepper to taste

Instructions:
a) In a small bowl, whisk together the BBQ sauce, honey, soy sauce, garlic, ginger, salt, and pepper.
b) Place the chicken wings in a large resealable plastic bag and pour the marinade over them. Seal the bag and toss to coat the wings.
c) Marinate in the refrigerator for at least 2 hours, or overnight for best results.
d) Preheat grill to medium-high heat. Remove wings from the marinade and discard the remaining marinade.
e) Grill the wings for about 15-20 minutes, turning occasionally, until they are cooked through and crispy.
f) Serve hot with your favorite dipping sauce.

2. Buffalo Chicken Dip

Ingredients:

- 2 cups shredded cooked chicken
- 8 oz cream cheese, softened
- 1/2 cup hot sauce
- 1/2 cup ranch dressing
- 1 cup shredded cheddar cheese
- 1/4 cup blue cheese crumbles (optional)
- Tortilla chips or celery sticks, for serving

Instructions:

a) Preheat oven to 350°F.

b) In a large mixing bowl, combine the shredded chicken, cream cheese, hot sauce, and ranch dressing. Stir until well combined.

c) Spread the mixture into a 9-inch baking dish and sprinkle with shredded cheddar cheese and blue cheese crumbles (if using).

d) Bake for 20-25 minutes, or until hot and bubbly.

e) Serve hot with tortilla chips or celery sticks.

3. Jalapeño Poppers

Ingredients:

- 12 jalapeño peppers, halved lengthwise and seeded
- 8 oz cream cheese, softened
- 1/2 cup shredded cheddar cheese
- 1/4 cup grated Parmesan cheese
- 1/4 tsp garlic powder
- 1/4 tsp onion powder
- Salt and pepper to taste
- 12 slices bacon, halved

Instructions:

a) Preheat oven to 400°F.

b) In a mixing bowl, combine the cream cheese, cheddar cheese, Parmesan cheese, garlic powder, onion powder, salt, and pepper. Mix until well combined.

c) Spoon the cheese mixture evenly into the jalapeño halves.

d) Wrap each jalapeño half with a slice of bacon and secure with a toothpick.

e) Place the jalapeño poppers on a baking sheet and bake for 20-25 minutes, or until the bacon is crispy and the filling is hot and bubbly.

f) Serve hot.

4. Alkaline Baba Ganoush

Servings: 4
Preparation Time: 30 Minutes

INGREDIENTS:

- 1 Large aubergine
- A handful of parsley
- 1-2 cloves of garlic
- Juice of 2 lemons
- 2 tablespoons of tahini
- Salt & black pepper to taste

INSTRUCTIONS:

a) Preheat the grill to medium-high and cook the aubergine whole for around half an hour.

b) Cut into it and scrape the insides off with a spoon, then place the flesh in a strainer.

c) Blend until smooth.

5. <u>Courgette and Chickpea Hummus</u>

Servings: 4
Preparation Time: 30 Minutes

INGREDIENTS:

- 1 can of chickpeas, drained and rinsed
- 1 garlic clove, chopped
- 1 green courgette, chopped
- Handful chopped parsley
- Handful chopped basil
- Himalayan or Sea Salt
- Freshly ground black pepper
- 4 tablespoons olive oil
- A squeeze of fresh lemon juice

INSTRUCTIONS:

a) Blend everything.

6. Lemony Chickpea and Tahini Hummus

Servings: 2
Preparation Time: 10 Minutes

INGREDIENTS:
- Lemon juice from 1/2 a lemon
- 1 can dried chickpeas, soaked
- 1 clove of garlic
- 1 tablespoon of tahini
- 1 tablespoon of olive oil

INSTRUCTIONS:
a) Blend everything until smooth.

7. Garlicky Chickpea Hummus

Servings: 2
Preparation Time: 10 Minutes

INGREDIENTS:

- 2 cloves of garlic
- 1 can of chick peas
- 1 tablespoon of Tahini
- Lemon juice from 1 Lemon
- 1 tablespoon olive oil

INSTRUCTIONS:

a) In a mixing bowl, blend all ingredients.

8. Spicy Pumpkin & Cream Cheese Dip

Total Time for Preparation: 5 minutes
Servings: 4 to 6 servings

INGREDIENTS

- 8 ounces Cream Cheese
- 15 ounces unsweetened canned pumpkin
- 1 teaspoon cinnamon
- 1/4 teaspoon allspice
- 1/4 teaspoon nutmeg
- 10 pecans, smashed

INSTRUCTIONS

a) Whip the Cream Cheese and canned pumpkin together in a mixer until creamy.
b) Stir in the cinnamon, allspice, nutmeg, and pecans until thoroughly combined. Before serving, chill for one hour in the refrigerator.

NUTRITION: Calories 227| Fat 19g (Saturated 4g) | Cholesterol 0mg| Sodium 275mg| Carbohydrate 12g| Dietary Fiber 6g| Protein 4g.

9. <u>Cream Cheese and Honey Dip</u>

Total Time for Preparation: 5 minutes
Servings: 2 servings

INGREDIENTS

a) 2 ounces Cream Cheese
b) 2 tablespoons honey
c) 1/4 cup squeezed orange juice
d) 1/2 teaspoon ground cinnamon

INSTRUCTIONS

a) Blend everything until smooth.

NUTRITION: Calories 160| Fat 8g (Saturated 2g) | Cholesterol 0mg| Sodium 136mg| Carbohydrate 22g| Dietary Fiber 0g| Protein 1g.

10. <u>Garlicky Alkaline Guacamole</u>

Total Time for Preparation: 10 minutes
Servings: 6 servings

INGREDIENTS
- 2 avocados, pitted
- 1 tomato, seeded and finely chopped
- 1/2 tablespoon fresh lime juice
- 1/2 small yellow onions, finely chopped
- 2 garlic cloves, pressed
- 1/4 teaspoon sea salt
- Dash of pepper
- Minced fresh cilantro leaf

INSTRUCTIONS
a) Using a potato masher, mash the avocados in a small bowl.
b) Serve immediately after mixing the additional INGREDIENTS into the mashed avocados.

NUTRITION: Calories 97| Fat 8g (Saturated 2g) | Cholesterol 0mg| Sodium 97mg| Carbohydrate 6g| Dietary Fiber 5g| Protein 1g.

11. <u>Alkaline Jalapeño Salsa</u>

Total Time for Preparation: 10 minutes
Servings: 4 servings

INGREDIENTS
- 4 medium tomatoes, peeled and diced
- 1/4 cup chopped red onion
- Jalapeño pepper, seeded and finely chopped
- 1 tablespoon cold-pressed olive oil
- 1 teaspoon sea salt
- 1 teaspoon cumin
- 1 teaspoon minced garlic
- Fresh parsley

INSTRUCTIONS
a) Blend all of the ingredients.

NUTRITION: Calories 73| Fat 4g (Saturated 1g) | Cholesterol 0mg| Sodium 582mg| Carbohydrate 9g| Dietary Fiber 1g| Protein 1g.

12.   <u>Caviar Heart Kisses</u>

Ingredients:

- 1 Cucumber, scrubbed and trimmed
- 1/3 cup Sour Cream
- 1 ts Dried dill weed
- Freshly ground black pepper to taste
- 1 Jar red salmon caviar
- Fresh dill sprigs
- 8 Thin slices whole-wheat bread
- Butter or margarine

Directions:

a) Slice cucumber into 1/4-inch rounds.

b) In a small bowl, combine sour cream, dried dill and pepper. Place one teaspoon of the sour cream mixture on each cucumber slice. Garnish each with about 1/2-teaspoon caviar and a dill sprig.

c) Cut bread slices with heart-shaped cookie cutter. Toast and butter. Place cucumber slices in centre of serving plate and surround with toast hearts.

13.   <u>Burrito bites</u>

Ingredients:

- 1 can Diced Tomatoes
- 1 cup Instant rice
- ⅓ cup Water
- 1 Green pepper, diced
- 2 Green onions, sliced
- 2 cups Shredded cheddar cheese, divided
- 1 can Ranch Style Refried Beans (16 oz)
- 10 Flour tortillas (6-7")
- 1 cup Salsa

Directions:

a) Preheat oven to 350'F. Spray a 9x12" baking dish with PAM; set aside.

b) In a medium saucepan, combine rice and water; heat to a boil.

c) Reduce heat, cover and simmer 1 minute. Remove from heat and let sit 5 minutes or until all liquid is absorbed. Stir in pepper, onions and 1 cup cheese.

d) Spread about 3 tablespoons beans over each tortilla to within $\frac{1}{8}$" from edge. Layer rice mixture over beans; roll up. Place seam side down in prepared baking dish; cover with foil.

e) Bake in preheated oven 25 minutes or until hot. Cut tortillas into 4 pieces and place on platter. Top with salsa and cheese. Top with salsa and cheese. Return to oven and bake 5 minutes or until cheese melts.

14.   <u>Chicken nut bites</u>

Ingredients:

- 1 cup Chicken broth
- ½ cup Butter
- 1 cup Flour
- 1 tablespoon Parsley
- 2 teaspoons Seasoned salt
- 2 teaspoons Worcestershire Sauce
- 34 teaspoons Celery seed
- ½ teaspoon Paprika
- ⅛ teaspoon Cayenne
- 4 large Eggs
- 2 Chicken breasts, poached, skinned
- ¼ cup Toasted almonds

Directions:

15. Preheat oven to 400 degrees. In a heavy pan, combine broth and butter, and bring to a boil. Whisk in flour and seasoning.
16. Cook, whisking rapidly, until mixture leaves sides of pan and forms a smooth, compact ball. Remove from heat. Add eggs one at a time, beating well until mixture is shiny. Stir in chicken and almonds.
17. Drop by rounded teaspoonfuls onto greased baking sheets. Bake for 15 minutes. Freeze after baking.

15.   <u>Buffalo chicken fingers</u>

Ingredients:

- 2 cups almond flour
- 1 teaspoon salt
- 1 teaspoon black pepper
- 1 teaspoon dried parsley
- 2 large eggs
- 2 tablespoons full-fat canned coconut milk
- 2 pounds chicken tenders
- 1 1/2 cups Frank's Red-hot Buffalo sauce

Directions:

a) Preheat oven to 350°F.

b) Combine almond flour, salt, pepper, and parsley in a medium bowl and set aside.

c) Beat eggs and coconut milk together in a separate medium bowl.

d) Dip each chicken tender into egg mixture and then coat completely with almond flour mixture. Arrange coated tenders in a single layer on a baking sheet.

e) Bake 30 minutes, flipping once during cooking. Remove from oven and allow to cool 5 minutes.

f) Place chicken tenders in a large bowl and add buffalo sauce. Toss to coat completely.

16.   <u>Meatloaf muffins</u>

Ingredients:

- 1 pound ground beef
- 1 cup chopped spinach
- 1 large egg, lightly beaten
- 1/2 cup shredded mozzarella cheese
- 1/4 cup grated Parmesan cheese
- 1/4 cup chopped yellow onion
- 2 tablespoons seeded and minced jalapeño pepper

Directions:

a) Preheat oven to 350°F. Lightly grease each well of a muffin tin.

b) Combine all ingredients in large bowl and use your hands to mix.

c) Scoop an equal portion of meat mixture into each muffin tin and press down lightly. Bake 45 minutes or until internal temperature reaches 165°F.

17. Bacon avocado bites

Ingredients:

- 2 large avocados, peeled and pitted
- 8 slices no-sugar-added bacon
- 1/$_2$ teaspoon garlic salt

Directions:

a) Preheat oven to 425°F. Line a cookie sheet with parchment paper.

b) Cut each avocado into 8 equal-sized slices, making 16 slices total.

c) Cut each piece of bacon in half. Wrap a half slice of bacon around each piece of avocado. Sprinkle with garlic salt.

d) Place avocado on cookie sheet and bake 15 minutes. Turn oven to broil and continue to cook another 2–3 minutes until bacon becomes crispy.

18.   Pizza bites

Ingredients:

- 24 slices sugar-free pepperoni
- 1/₂ cup marinara sauce
- 1/₂ cup shredded mozzarella cheese

Directions:

A) TURN ON OVEN BROILER.

B) LINE A BAKING SHEET WITH PARCHMENT PAPER AND LAY OUT PEPPERONI SLICES IN A SINGLE LAYER.

C) PUT 1 TEASPOON MARINARA SAUCE ON EACH PEPPERONI SLICE AND SPREAD OUT WITH A SPOON. ADD 1 TEASPOON MOZZARELLA CHEESE ON TOP OF MARINARA.

D) PUT BAKING SHEET IN THE OVEN AND BROIL 3 MINUTES OR UNTIL CHEESE IS MELTED AND SLIGHTLY BROWN.

E) REMOVE FROM BAKING SHEET AND TRANSFER TO A PAPER TOWEL-LINED BAKING SHEET TO ABSORB EXCESS GREASE.

19.   <u>Bacon and scallion bites</u>

Ingredients:

- 1/3 cup almond meal
- 1 tablespoon unsalted butter, melted
- 1 (8-ounce) package cream cheese, softened to room temperature
- 1 tablespoon bacon grease
- 1 large egg
- 4 slices no-sugar-added bacon, cooked, cooled, and crumbled into bits
- 1 large green onion, tops only, thinly sliced
- 1 clove garlic, minced
- 1/8 teaspoon black pepper

Directions:

A) PREHEAT OVEN TO 325°F.

B) IN A SMALL MIXING BOWL, COMBINE ALMOND MEAL AND BUTTER.

C) LINE 6 CUPS OF A STANDARD-SIZED MUFFIN TIN WITH CUPCAKE LINERS. EQUALLY DIVIDE ALMOND MEAL MIXTURE AMONG CUPS AND PRESS INTO THE BOTTOM GENTLY WITH THE BACK OF A TEASPOON. BAKE IN OVEN 10 MINUTES, THEN REMOVE.

D) WHILE THE CRUST IS BAKING, THOROUGHLY COMBINE CREAM CHEESE AND BACON GREASE IN A MEDIUM MIXING BOWL WITH A HAND MIXER. ADD EGG AND BLEND UNTIL COMBINED.

E) FOLD BACON, ONION, GARLIC, AND PEPPER INTO CREAM CHEESE MIXTURE WITH A SPATULA.

F) DIVIDE MIXTURE AMONG CUPS, RETURN TO OVEN, AND BAKE ANOTHER 30-35 MINUTES UNTIL CHEESE SETS. EDGES MAY BE SLIGHTLY BROWNED. TO TEST DONENESS, INSERT TOOTHPICK INTO CENTER. IF IT COMES OUT CLEAN, CHEESECAKE IS DONE.

G) LET COOL 5 MINUTES AND SERVE.

20.   <u>Bacon-wrapped chicken bites</u>

Ingredients:

- 3/4 pound boneless, skinless chicken breast, cut into 1" cubes
- 1/2 teaspoon salt
- 1/2 teaspoon black pepper
- 5 slices no-sugar-added bacon

Directions:

A) PREHEAT OVEN TO 375°F.

B) TOSS CHICKEN WITH SALT AND PEPPER.

C) CUT EACH SLICE OF BACON INTO 3 PIECES AND WRAP EACH PIECE OF CHICKEN IN A PIECE OF BACON. SECURE WITH A TOOTHPICK.

D) PUT WRAPPED CHICKEN ON A BROILER RACK AND BAKE 30 MINUTES, TURNING OVER HALFWAY THROUGH COOKING. TURN OVEN TO BROIL AND BROIL 3-4 MINUTES OR UNTIL BACON IS CRISPY.

21.   <u>Bacon-oyster bites</u>

Ingredients:

- 8 SLICES BACON
- $\frac{1}{2}$ CUP HERBED SEASONED STUFFING
- 1 CAN (5-OZ) OYSTERS; CHOPPED
- $\frac{1}{4}$ CUP WATER

Directions:

A) PREHEAT OVEN TO 350Ø. CUT BACON SLICES IN HALF AND COOK SLIGHTLY. DO NOT OVERCOOK.

B) BACON MUST BE SOFT ENOUGH TO ROLL EASILY AROUND BALLS. COMBINE STUFFING, OYSTERS AND WATER.

C) ROLL INTO BITE-SIZED BALLS, APPROXIMATELY 16.

D) WRAP BALLS IN BACON. BAKE AT 350Ø FOR 25 MINUTES. SERVE WARM.

22.   Buffalo cauliflower bites

Ingredients:

- 1 cup almond meal
- 1 teaspoon granulated garlic
- $1/2$ teaspoon dried parsley
- $1/2$ teaspoon salt
- 1 large egg
- 1 large head cauliflower, cut into bite-sized florets
- $1/2$ cup Frank's Red-hot sauce
- $1/4$ cup ghee

Directions:

A) PREHEAT OVEN TO 400°F. LINE A BAKING SHEET WITH PARCHMENT PAPER.

B) COMBINE ALMOND MEAL, GARLIC, PARSLEY, AND SALT IN A LARGE SEALABLE PLASTIC BAG AND SHAKE TO MIX.

C) WHISK EGG IN A LARGE BOWL. ADD CAULIFLOWER AND TOSS TO COAT COMPLETELY.

D) TRANSFER CAULIFLOWER TO BAG FILLED WITH ALMOND MEAL MIXTURE AND TOSS TO COAT.

E) ARRANGE CAULIFLOWER IN A SINGLE LAYER ON BAKING SHEET AND BAKE 30 MINUTES OR UNTIL SOFTENED AND SLIGHTLY BROWNED.

F) WHILE CAULIFLOWER IS BAKING, COMBINE HOT SAUCE AND GHEE IN A SMALL SAUCEPAN OVER LOW HEAT.

G) WHEN CAULIFLOWER IS COOKED, COMBINE CAULIFLOWER WITH HOT SAUCE MIXTURE IN A LARGE MIXING BOWL AND TOSS TO COAT.

23. <u>Chocolate Chili Mini Churros</u>

Ingredients:

- 1 cup water
- 1/2 cup coconut oil or vegan butter
- 1 cup flour
- 1/4 teaspoons salt
- 3 eggs beaten
- Cinnamon Sugar Mixture
- 1/2 cup sugar1 tablespoon cinnamon

Directions:

a) Pre-heat oven to 400Combine water, coconut oil/butter and salt in a pot and bring to a boil.

b) Whisk in flour, stirring quickly until mixture turns into a ball.

c) Slowly stir in the eggs a little at a time, mixing continuously to make sure the eggs don't scramble.

d) Allow batter to cool slightly, and then transfer to your piping bag.

e) Pipe 3 inch long churros into rows on your greased baking sheet.

f) Bake in the oven for 10 minutes at 400 degrees and then broil on high for 1-2 minutes until your churros are golden brown.

g) Meanwhile, mix together cinnamon and sugar in a small dish.

h) Once churros are out of the oven, roll them into the cinnamon and sugar mix until fully coated. Set aside.

24. <u>Bouillabaisse bites</u>

Ingredients:

- 24 mediums Shrimp -- peeled and
- Deveined
- 24 mediums Sea scallops
- 2 cups Tomato sauce
- 1 can Minced clams (6-1/2 oz)
- 1 tablespoon Pernod
- 20 Milliliters
- 1 Bay leaf
- 1 teaspoon Basil
- $\frac{1}{2}$ teaspoon Salt
- $\frac{1}{2}$ teaspoon Freshly ground pepper
- Garlic -- minced
- Saffron

Directions:

a) Skewer shrimp and scallops on 8-inch bamboo skewers, using 1 shrimp and 1 scallop per skewer; wrap tail of shrimp around scallop.

b) Mix tomato sauce, clams, Pernod, garlic, bay leaf, basil, salt, pepper and saffron together in saucepan. Bring mixture to boil.

c) Arrange skewered fish in shallow baking dish.

d) Drizzle sauce over skewers. Bake, uncovered, at 350 degrees for 25 minutes. Makes 24

25.   <u>Cauliflower cups</u>

Ingredients:

- 11/2 cups cauliflower rice
- 1/4 cup diced onion
- 1/2 cup shredded pepper jack cheese
- 1/2 teaspoon dried oregano
- 1/2 teaspoon dried basil
- 1/2 teaspoon salt
- 1 large egg, lightly beaten

Directions:

a) Preheat oven to 350°F.

b) Combine all ingredients in a large mixing bowl and stir to incorporate.

c) Scoop mixture into the wells of a mini muffin tin and pack lightly.

d) Bake 30 minutes or until cups start to crisp. Allow to cool slightly and remove from tin.

26.   <u>Mac and Cheese Cups</u>

Ingredients:

- 8 oz elbow macaroni
- 2 tbsp salted butter
- 1/4 teaspoons paprika (use smoked paprika if you have it)
- 2 tbsp flour
- 1/2 cup whole milk
- 8 oz sharp cheddar cheese grated
- chopped chives or scallions for garnish
- butter for greasing the pan

Directions:

a) Grease a non-stick: mini muffin pan very well with butter or non-stick: cooking spray. Preheat the oven to 400 degrees F.

b) Bring a pot of salted water to a boil over high heat, then cook the pasta for 2 minutes less than the package says.

c) Melt the butter and add the paprika. Add the flour and stir the mixture around for 2 minutes. While whisking, add the milk.

d) Remove the pot from the heat and add the cheeses and drained pasta, stirring it all together until the cheese and sauce are well distributed.

e) Portion your mac and cheese into the muffin cups, either with a spoon or a 3-tbsp cookie scoop.

f) Bake the mac and cheese cups for 15 minutes, until bubbling and gooey.

27.   <u>Bologna quiche cups</u>

Ingredients:

- 12 Slices bologna
- 2 Eggs
- $\frac{1}{2}$ cup Biscuit mix
- $\frac{1}{2}$ cup Shredded sharp cheese
- $\frac{1}{4}$ cup Sweet pickle relish
- 1 cup Milk

Directions:

e) Place bologna slices in lightly greased muffin tins to form cups.

f) Mix together remaining ingredients. Pour into bologna cups.

g) Bake at (400F) for 20-25 minutes or until golden.

28.   Muffin prosciutto cup

Ingredients:

- 1 slice prosciutto (about 1/2 ounce)
- 1 medium egg yolk
- 3 tablespoons diced Brie
- 2 tablespoons diced mozzarella cheese
- 3 tablespoons grated Parmesan cheese

Directions:

a) Preheat oven to 350°F. Take out a muffin tin with wells about 21/2" wide and 11/2" deep.

b) Fold prosciutto slice in half so it becomes almost square. Place it in muffin tin well to line it completely.

c) Place egg yolk into prosciutto cup.

d) Add cheeses on top of egg yolk gently without breaking it.

e) Bake about 12 minutes until yolk is cooked and warm but still runny.

f) Let cool 10 minutes before removing from muffin tin.

29.   Brussels sprouts cups

Ingredients:

- 12 mediums Brussels sprouts
- 6 ounces Yukon Gold potatoes
- 2 tablespoons Skim milk
- 1 tablespoon Olive oil
- $\frac{1}{8}$ teaspoon Salt
- 2 ounces Smoked trout, skinned
- 1 Roasted red pepper, cut into 2 inch by 1/8 inch strips

Directions:

a) Preheat oven to 350

b) Trim stems, cut in half lengthwise, remove core leaving cups of darker green leaves.

c) Steam sprout cups for 6 minutes or until they're tender when pierced with a sharp knife and are still bright green.

d) Drain upside down on paper towels. Cook potatoes until tender , drain, adOd milk, olive oil and salt.

e) Beat until smooth. Gently fold in trout. +$\frac{1}{4}$> spoon into shells and place pepper strips on top.

30. <u>Endive cups</u>

Ingredients:

- 1 large hard-boiled egg, peeled
- 2 tablespoons canned tuna in olive oil, drained
- 2 tablespoons avocado pulp
- 1 teaspoon fresh lime juice
- 1 tablespoon mayonnaise
- $1/8$ teaspoon sea salt
- $1/8$ teaspoon black pepper
- 4 Belgian endive leaves, washed and dried

Directions:

a) In a small food processor, mix all ingredients except endive until well blended.

b) Scoop 1 tablespoon tuna mixture onto each endive cup.

31. <u>Taco cups</u>

Ingredients:

- Chili powder,Cumin, paprika
- Salt, black pepper
- 1/4 teaspoon dried oregano
- 1/4 teaspoon crushed red pepper flakes
- 1/4 teaspoon granulated garlic
- 1/4 teaspoon granulated onion
- 1 pound 75% lean ground beef
- 8 (1-ounce) slices sharp Cheddar cheese
- 1/2 cup no-sugar-added salsa
- 1/4 cup chopped cilantro
- 3 tablespoons Frank's Red-hot sauce

Directions:

a) Preheat oven to 375°F. Line a baking sheet with parchment paper.

b) Combine spices in a small bowl and stir to mix. Cook ground beef in a medium skillet over medium-high heat. When beef is almost done cooking, add spice mixture and stir to coat completely. Remove from heat and set aside.

c) Arrange Cheddar cheese slices on lined baking sheet. Bake in preheated oven 5 minutes or until starting to brown. Allow to cool 3 minutes and then peel from baking sheet and transfer each slice to the well of a muffin tin, forming a cup. Allow to cool.

d) Scoop equal amounts of meat into each cup and top with 1 tablespoon of salsa. Sprinkle cilantro and hot sauce on top.

32.   Ham 'n' cheddar cups

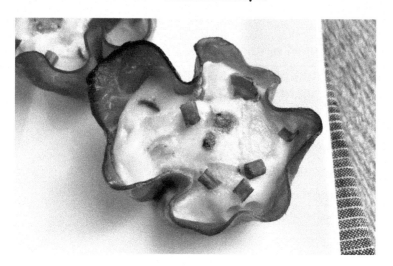

Ingredients:

- 2 cups All-purpose flour
- $\frac{1}{4}$ cup Sugar
- 2 teaspoons Baking powder
- 1 teaspoon Salt
- $\frac{1}{4}$ teaspoon Pepper
- 6 Eggs
- 1 cup Milk
- $\frac{1}{2}$ pounds Fully cooked ham; cubed
- $\frac{1}{2}$ pounds Cheddar cheese; diced or shredded
- $\frac{1}{2}$ pounds Sliced bacon; cooked and crumbled
- 1 small Onion; finely chopped

Directions:

a) In bowl, combine the flour, sugar, baking powder, salt and pepper. Beat eggs and milk; stir into dry ingredients until well mixed. Stir in ham, cheese, bacon and onion.

b) Fill well-greased muffin cups three-fourths full.

c) Bake at 350° for 45 minutes. Cool for 10 minutes before removing to a wire rack.

33.   Cocktail party shrimp

Ingredients:

- 1 Bunch scallions/shallots
- ½ large Bunch parsley
- 2 cans Whole pimentos
- 2 larges Pods garlic
- 3 Parts salad oil to 1 part
- White vinegar
- Salt
- Pepper
- Dry mustard
- Red pepper
- 5 pounds Boiled shelled cleaned
- Shrimp or defrosted frozen

Directions:

a) Chop vegetables fine in a food processor or blender. Add to oil/ vinegar mixture. Mix well. Season to taste with other seasoning.

b) Pour mixture over shrimp, turn several times. Refrigerate for at least 24 hours, mixing occasionally. Drain liquid to serve. Serve with toothpicks.

34.   Cocktail kebabs

Ingredients:

- 8 large Shrimp, cooked
- 2 Green onions, trimmed
- $\frac{1}{2}$ Red bell pepper, seeded, cut in thin strips
- 8 smalls Ripe or green olives
- 1bGarlic clove, crushed
- 2 tablespoons Lemon juice
- 2 tablespoons Olive oil
- 1 teaspoon Sugar
- 1 teaspoon Coarsely ground mustard
- $\frac{1}{4}$ teaspoon Creamed horseradish

Directions:

a) Remove heads and body shells from shrimp but leave on tail shells.

b) Devein shrimp by removing black spinal cord. Cut each green onion in 4 daisies. Put shrimp, green onions, bell pepper and olives in a bowl.

c) Mix garlic, lemon juice, olive oil, sugar, mustard and horseradish.

d) Pour over shrimp mixture, cover and marinate at least 2 hours, stirring occasionally. Remove ingredients from marinade and thread equally on 8 wooden picks. Drain on paper towels.

35.   <u>Cocktail water chestnuts</u>

Ingredients:

- 8½ ounce Can of water chestnuts
- Save 1/2 cup of liquid
- ½ cup Vinegar
- 12 slices Bacon, halved
- ¼ cup Brown sugar
- ¼ cup Catsup

Directions:

a) Marinate chestnuts in liquid and vinegar for 1 hour. Drain.
b) Mix brown sugar and catsup; then spread on bacon. Roll chestnuts in bacon. Fasten with toothpicks.
c) Broil until bacon is crisp.

36.   Cocktail wieners

Ingredients:

- ¾ cup Prepared mustard
- 1 cup Currant jelly
- 1 pounds (8-10) frankfurters Wieners

Directions:

a) Mix mustard and currant jelly in chafing dish or double boiler.

b) Diagonally slice frankfurters in bite size pieces. Add to sauce and heat through.

37. Cocktail rye hors d'oeuvres

Ingredients:

- 1 cup mayonnaise
- 1 cup Shredded sharp cheddar cheese
- $\frac{1}{2}$ cup Parmesan cheese
- 1 cup Sliced green onions
- Cocktail rye bread slices

Directions:

a) Combine the mayo, cheeses and onions. Mound about $1\frac{1}{2}$ tbsp (or more) onto each bread slice.

b) Place on a baking sheet and put under broiler until bubbly, watching to make sure they don't burn.

38.   <u>Bacon jalapeño balls</u>

Ingredients:

- 5 slices no-sugar-added bacon, cooked, fat reserved
- 1/4 cup plus 2 tablespoons (3 ounces) cream cheese
- 2 tablespoons reserved bacon fat
- 1 teaspoon seeded and finely chopped jalapeño pepper
- 1 tablespoon finely chopped cilantro

Directions:

1. ON A CUTTING BOARD, CHOP BACON INTO SMALL CRUMBS.

2. IN A SMALL BOWL, COMBINE CREAM CHEESE, BACON FAT, JALAPEÑO, AND CILANTRO; MIX WELL WITH A FORK.

3. FORM MIXTURE INTO 6 BALLS.

4. PLACE BACON CRUMBLES ON A MEDIUM PLATE AND ROLL INDIVIDUAL BALLS THROUGH TO COAT EVENLY.

5. SERVE IMMEDIATELY OR REFRIGERATE UP TO 3 DAYS.

39.   <u>Avocado prosciutto balls</u>

Ingredients:

- 1/2 cup macadamia nuts
- 1/2 large avocado, peeled and pitted (about 4 ounces pulp)
- 1 ounce cooked prosciutto, crumbled
- 1/4 teaspoon black pepper

Directions:

A) IN A SMALL FOOD PROCESSOR, PULSE MACADAMIA NUTS UNTIL EVENLY CRUMBLED. DIVIDE IN HALF.

B) IN A SMALL BOWL, COMBINE AVOCADO, HALF THE MACADAMIA NUTS, PROSCIUTTO CRUMBLES, AND PEPPER AND MIX WELL WITH A FORK.

C) FORM MIXTURE INTO 6 BALLS.

D) PLACE REMAINING CRUMBLED MACADAMIA NUTS ON A MEDIUM PLATE AND ROLL INDIVIDUAL BALLS THROUGH TO COAT EVENLY.

E) SERVE IMMEDIATELY.

40. <u>Barbecue balls</u>

Ingredients:

- 4 ounces (1/₂ cup) cream cheese
- 4 tablespoons bacon fat
- 1/₂ teaspoon smoke flavor
- 2 drops stevia glycerite
- 1/₈ teaspoon apple cider vinegar
- 1 tablespoon sweet smoked chili powder

Directions:

A) IN A SMALL FOOD PROCESSOR, PROCESS ALL INGREDIENTS EXCEPT CHILI POWDER UNTIL THEY FORM A SMOOTH CREAM, ABOUT 30 SECONDS.

B) SCRAPE MIXTURE AND TRANSFER INTO A SMALL BOWL, THEN REFRIGERATE 2 HOURS.

C) FORM INTO 6 BALLS WITH THE AID OF A SPOON.

D) SPRINKLE BALLS WITH CHILI POWDER, ROLLING AROUND TO COAT ALL SIDES.

E) SERVE IMMEDIATELY OR REFRIGERATE UP TO 3 DAYS.

41. <u>Bacon maple pancake balls</u>

Ingredients:

- 5 slices no-sugar-added bacon, cooked
- 4 ounces (1/2 cup) cream cheese
- 1/2 teaspoon maple flavor
- 1/4 teaspoon salt
- 3 tablespoons crushed pecans

Directions:

A) ON A CUTTING BOARD, CHOP BACON INTO SMALL CRUMBS.

B) IN A SMALL BOWL, COMBINE CREAM CHEESE AND BACON CRUMBLES WITH MAPLE FLAVOR AND SALT; MIX WELL WITH A FORK.

C) FORM MIXTURE INTO 6 BALLS.

D) PLACE CRUSHED PECANS ON A MEDIUM PLATE AND ROLL INDIVIDUAL BALLS THROUGH TO COAT EVENLY.

E) SERVE IMMEDIATELY OR REFRIGERATE UP TO 3 DAYS.

42. Sunbutter balls

Ingredients:

- 6 tablespoons mascarpone cheese
- 3 tablespoons no-sugar-added sunflower seed butter
- 6 tablespoons coconut oil, softened
- 3 tablespoons unsweetened shredded coconut flakes

Directions:

A) IN A MEDIUM BOWL, MIX MASCARPONE CHEESE, SUNFLOWER SEED BUTTER, AND COCONUT OIL UNTIL A SMOOTH PASTE FORMS.

B) SHAPE PASTE INTO WALNUT-SIZED BALLS. IF MIXTURE IS TOO STICKY, PLACE IN REFRIGERATOR 15 MINUTES BEFORE FORMING BALLS.

C) SPREAD COCONUT FLAKES ON A MEDIUM PLATE AND ROLL INDIVIDUAL BALLS THROUGH TO COAT EVENLY.

43.   <u>Brazilian onion bites</u>

Ingredients:

- 1 small Onion 1/4'd lengthwise
- 6 tablespoons Mayonnaise
- Salt and pepper
- 6 Bread slices -- crusts removed
- 3 tablespoons Parmesan cheese -- grated

Directions:

a) Preheat the oven to 350. Mix the onion with 5 tbsp of the mayonnaise and salt and pepper to taste. Set aside. Spread 3 slices of bread on one side with the remaining mayonnaise. Cut these into quarters.

b) Cut the remaining 3 slices of bread into quarters and spread each square evenly with the onion mixture. Top with the reserved bread squares, mayonnaise side up. Place these on a baking sheet and sprinkle the tops generously with parmesan cheese.

c) Bake until lightly golden and slightly puffy, about 15 minutes. Serve immediately.

44.   Pizza balls

Ingredients:

- 1/4 cup (2 ounces) fresh mozzarella cheese
- 2 ounces (1/4 cup) cream cheese
- 1 tablespoon olive oil
- 1 teaspoon tomato paste
- 6 large kalamata olives, pitted
- 12 fresh basil leaves

Directions:

A) IN A SMALL FOOD PROCESSOR, PROCESS ALL INGREDIENTS EXCEPT BASIL UNTIL THEY FORM A SMOOTH CREAM, ABOUT 30 SECONDS.

B) FORM MIXTURE INTO 6 BALLS WITH THE AID OF A SPOON.

C) PLACE 1 BASIL LEAF ON TOP AND BOTTOM OF EACH BALL AND SECURE WITH A TOOTHPICK.

D) SERVE IMMEDIATELY OR REFRIGERATE UP TO 3 DAYS.

45. <u>Olive and feta balls</u>

Ingredients:

- 2 ounces (1/4 cup) cream cheese
- 1/4 cup (2 ounces) feta cheese
- 12 large kalamata olives, pitted
- 1/8 teaspoon finely chopped fresh thyme
- 1/8 teaspoon fresh lemon zest

Directions:

a) In a small food processor, process all ingredients until they form a coarse dough, about 30 seconds.

b) Scrape mixture and transfer to a small bowl, then refrigerate 2 hours.

c) Form into 6 balls with the aid of a spoon.

d) Serve immediately or refrigerate up to 3 days.

46.   Brie hazelnut balls

Ingredients:

- 1/2 cup (4 ounces) Brie
- 1/4 cup toasted hazelnuts
- 1/8 teaspoon finely chopped fresh thyme

Directions:

a) In a small food processor, process all ingredients until they form a coarse dough, about 30 seconds.

b) Scrape mixture, transfer to a small bowl, and refrigerate 2 hours.

c) Form into 6 balls with the aid of a spoon.

d) Serve immediately or refrigerate up to 3 days.

47.   <u>Curried tuna balls</u>

Ingredients:

- 1/4 cup plus 2 tablespoons (3 ounces) tuna in oil, drained
- 2 ounces (1/4 cup) cream cheese
- 1/4 teaspoon curry powder, divided
- 2 tablespoons crumbled macadamia nuts

Directions:

a) In a small food processor, process tuna, cream cheese, and half the curry powder until they form a smooth cream, about 30 seconds.

b) Form mixture into 6 balls.

c) Place crumbled macadamia nuts and remaining curry powder on a medium plate and roll individual balls through to coat evenly.

48. Pork bombs

Ingredients:

- 8 slices no-sugar-added bacon
- 8 ounces Braunschweiger at room temperature
- 1/4 cup chopped pistachios
- 6 ounces (3/4 cup) cream cheese, softened to room temperature
- 1 teaspoon Dijon mustard

Directions:

a) Cook bacon in a medium skillet over medium heat until crisp, 5 minutes per side. Drain on paper towels and let cool. Once cooled, crumble into bacon-bit-sized pieces.

b) Place Braunschweiger with pistachios in a small food processor and pulse until just combined.

c) In a small mixing bowl, use a hand blender to whip cream cheese and Dijon mustard until combined and fluffy.

d) Divide meat mixture into 12 equal servings. Roll into balls and cover in a thin layer of cream cheese mixture.

e) Chill at least 1 hour. When ready to serve, place bacon bits on a medium plate, roll balls through to coat evenly, and enjoy.

f) Fat bombs can be refrigerated in an airtight container up to 4 days.

49.   <u>Salted caramel and brie balls</u>

Ingredients:

- 1/2 cup (4 ounces) roughly chopped Brie
- 1/4 cup salted macadamia nuts
- 1/2 teaspoon caramel flavor

Directions:

a) In a small food processor, process all ingredients until they form a coarse dough, about 30 seconds.
b) Form mixture into 6 balls with the aid of a spoon.
c) Serve immediately or refrigerate up to 3 days.

50. <u>Cocktail party meatballs</u>

Ingredients:

- $\frac{1}{4}$ cup Fat-free cottage cheese
- 2 Egg whites
- 2 teaspoons Worcestershire sauce
- $\frac{1}{2}$ cup Plus 2 tablespoons plain bread crumbs
- 8 ounces Ground turkey breast
- 6 ounces Turkey sausage; removed from casings
- 2 tablespoons Minced onions
- 2 tablespoons Minced green peppers
- $\frac{1}{2}$ cup Snipped fresh parsley and celery leaves

Directions:

a) Spray a cookie sheet with no-stick spray and set aside.

b) In a large bowl, stir together the cottage cheese, egg whites, Worcestershire sauce and $\frac{1}{2}$ cup of the bread crumbs. Stir in the turkey breast, turkey sausage, onions and green peppers.

c) Shape the poultry mixture into 32 meatballs. On a sheet of wax paper, combine the parsley, celery leaves and remaining 2 tablespoons bread crumbs. Roll the meatballs in the parsley mixture until coated evenly.

d) Transfer the meatballs to the prepared cookie sheet. Broil 3 to 4 inches from the heat for 10 to 12 minutes.

51. <u>Cocktail cheese balls</u>

Ingredients:

- 8 ounces cheese, softened
- $\frac{1}{4}$ cup Plain non-fat yogurt
- 4 ounces Shredded cheddar cheese
- 4 ounces Shredded reduced-fat Swiss cheese
- 2 teaspoons Grated onion
- 2 teaspoons Prepared horseradish
- 1 teaspoon Country-style Dijon Mustard
- $\frac{1}{4}$ cup Chopped fresh parsley

Directions:

a) Combine cheese and yogurt in a large mixing bowl; beat at medium speed of an electric mixer until smooth. Add cheddar cheese and next 4 ingredients; stir well. Cover and chill at least 1 hour.

b) Shape cheese mixture into a ball, and sprinkle with parsley. Press parsley gently into cheese ball. Wrap cheese ball in heavy-duty plastic wrap and chill. Serve with assorted unsalted crackers.

52. Crudites with relish

Ingredients:

- 2 teaspoons Olive oil
- 1 cup Finely chopped onion
- 1 tablespoon Chopped garlic
- 1 cup Canned crushed tomatoes
- 1 teaspoon Fresh lemon juice
- $\frac{1}{4}$ cup sun-dried tomatoes
- $\frac{1}{4}$ cup Pitted green olives; (about 10)
- $\frac{1}{4}$ cup (packed) fresh basil leaves
- 4 larges Drained canned artichoke hearts
- 2 tablespoons Chopped fresh parsley
- 2 tablespoons Toasted pine nuts
- Assorted vegetables

Directions:

a) Heat oil in medium non-stick: skillet over medium heat. Add onion and sauté until just beginning to soften, about 3 minutes. Add garlic; sauté 30 seconds. Stir in canned tomatoes and lemon juice. Bring to simmer. Remove from heat.

b) Combine sun-dried tomatoes and next 5 ingredients in processor. Using on/off turns, process until vegetables are finely chopped. Transfer to medium bowl. Stir in tomato mixture. Season with salt and pepper.

53. <u>Green and white crudites</u>

Ingredients:

54. ½ cup Plain yogurt
55. ½ cup Sour cream
56. ½ cup Mayonnaise
57. 1½ teaspoon White-wine vinegar; or to taste
58. 1½ teaspoon Coarse-grained mustard
59. 1 large Garlic clove; minced and mashed
60. 1 teaspoon Aniseed; crushed
61. 2 teaspoons Pernod; or to taste
62. 1½ tablespoon Minced tarragon leaves
63. 12 cups Assorted crudités

Directions:

a) In a bowl whisk together all ingredients except herbs with salt and pepper to taste. Chill dip, covered, at least 4 hours and up to 4 days. Just before serving, stir in tarragon and chervil.

b) Arrange crudités decoratively on a tiered serving plate or in a large basket and serve with dip.

54.   <u>Kohlrabi crudites</u>

Ingredients:

- ½ cup Soy sauce; light
- ½ cup Rice vinegar
- 1 teaspoon Sesame seeds; toasted
- 1 tablespoon Scallions; minced
- 4 cups Kohlrabi slices; cut into chunks

Directions:

a) Combine soy sauce, vinegar, sesame seeds and scallions.
b) Serve in a bowl surrounded by Kohlrabi chunks. Provide picks for eating.

55.   <u>Remoulade with vegetable crudites</u>

Ingredients:

- $\frac{1}{2}$ cup Creole or brown mustard
- $\frac{1}{2}$ cup Salad oil
- $\frac{1}{4}$ cup Catsup
- $\frac{1}{4}$ cup Cider vinegar
- $\frac{1}{4}$ teaspoon Tabasco sauce
- 2 tablespoons Finely chopped celery
- 2 tablespoons Finely chopped onion
- 2 tablespoons Finely chopped green pepper
- Cherry tomatoes
- Mushroom slices
- Cucumber slices
- Celery slices
- Carrot slices

Directions:

a) Combine mustard, oil, catsup, vinegar, Tabasco and chopped vegetables; cover and chill.
b) Serve dip with whole and sliced vegetables.

56. Skeleton crudite

Ingredients:
- 3 cups Low fat yogurt
- 1 cup Mayo
- $\frac{1}{2}$ cup Peach jam
- 1 teaspoon orange juice
- $\frac{1}{2}$ teaspoon Curry powder
- $\frac{1}{2}$ teaspoon Pepper.

Skeleton Ingredients
- 1 zucchini sliced in half lengthwise
- 1 yellow squash sliced in half
- 6 ribs celery cut in half lengthwise
- 1 cucumber sliced into wedges
- 1 carrot cut into sticks
- 10 baby carrot fingers
- 1 red pepper cut into2 inch thick strips
- 1 yellow pepper cut into 2 inch thick strips
- 2 broccoli florets/ 2 cauliflower florets
- 10 snow peas /2 cherry tomatoes
- 2 mushrooms/1 radish
- 4 green beans /2 yellow beans

Directions:
a) Stir together 3 cups low fat yogurt, 1 cup mayo, $\frac{1}{2}$ cup peach jam, 1 tablespoon orange juice, $\frac{1}{2}$ teaspoons curry powder and $\frac{1}{2}$ teaspoons pepper in a skull size bowl or scooped-out head of lettuce. Refrigerate.
b) Assemble skeleton

57. <u>Spicy winter crudite</u>

Ingredients:

- 1 Red onion; peeled sliced
- 1 Green pepper; seeded and cut
- 1 Red or yellow pepper; seeded and cut
- 1 Turnip; peeled and thinly
- 2 cups Cauliflower florets
- 2 cups Broccoli florets
- 1 cup Baby carrots; trimmed
- $\frac{1}{2}$ cup Thinly sliced radishes
- 2 tablespoons Salt
- $1\frac{1}{2}$ cup Olive oil
- 1 Yellow onion; peeled and finely; chopped
- $\frac{1}{8}$ teaspoon Saffron threads
- Pinch   Turmeric,Ground   cumin,black pepper,Paprika,Cayenne, Salt

Directions:

a) Place the prepared vegetables in a large bowl, sprinkle them with the 2 tablespoons of salt, and add the cold water.

b) The next day, drain and rinse the vegetables. Prepare the marinade by simmering the onion, spices, and salt in the olive oil for 10 minutes.

c) Spread the vegetables in a 9 x 13 inch dish. Pour the hot marinade over them.

d) Transfer to a decorative bowl to serve, either cold or at room temperature.

58. Tricolor crudites platter

Ingredients:

- $\frac{1}{4}$ cup Plus 1T red wine vinegar
- 3 tablespoons Dijon mustard
- $\frac{1}{2}$ cup Plus 2 T olive oil
- 2 tablespoons Minced fresh basil OR
- 2 teaspoons Dried basil
- 2 tablespoons Minced fresh chives or
- Green onions
- 1 teaspoon Minced fresh rosemary
- 2 Large cucumbers, peeled,
- 2 teaspoons Salt
- 2 Large raw beets, peeled, grated
- 2 Large carrots, peeled, grated
- 2 Large zucchini, grated
- 1 Bunch radishes, trimmed

Directions:

a) Whisk vinegar and Dijon mustard to blend in small bowl. Gradually whisk in olive oil. Mix in basil, chives and rosemary. Season with salt and pepper.

b) Toss cucumbers and 2 teaspoons salt in bowl. Let stand 1 hour. Rinse and drain well. Place cucumbers in small bowl; add enough dressing to coat.

c) Place beets, carrots and zucchini in separate bowls. Toss each vegetable with enough dressing to coat.

59.   <u>Mound vegetables on platter</u>

Ingredients:

- 1 cup Canned corn, drained
- 1 small Green onion, chopped
- 1 Green pepper, chopped
- 1 Garlic clove, minced
- 1 Fresh tomato, chopped
- $\frac{1}{4}$ cup Fresh parsley, chopped
- $\frac{1}{4}$ cup Extra virgin olive oil
- 2 tablespoons Balsamic vinegar
- Salt, Pepper
- 1 Scallion, chopped

Directions:

A) MIX CORN WITH ONION, GREEN PEPPER, GARLIC AND TOMATO. IN A SEPARATE SMALL BOWL OR CUP, MIX OLIVE OIL AND VINEGAR.

B) POUR OVER VEGETABLE, TOSS WITH PARSLEY; SEASON WITH SALT AND PEPPER. GARNISH EACH SERVING WITH SCALLIONS.

60.   Goat Cheese Guacamole

Serves: 4-6
Ingredients
- 2 avocados
- 3 ounces goat cheese
- zest from 2 limes
- lemon juice from 2 limes
- $\frac{3}{4}$ teaspoon garlic powder
- $\frac{3}{4}$ teaspoon onion powder
- $\frac{1}{2}$ teaspoon salt
- $\frac{1}{4}$ teaspoon red pepper flakes (optional)
- $\frac{1}{4}$ teaspoon pepper

Directions:

a) Add avocados to a food processor and blend until smooth. Add rest of ingredients and blend until incorporated.
b) Serve with chips.

61.   <u>Bavarian party dip/spread</u>

Yield: 1 1/4 pound

Ingredients:
- $\frac{1}{2}$ cup Onions, minced
- 1 pounds Braunschweiger
- 3 ounces Cream cheese
- $\frac{1}{4}$ teaspoon Black pepper

Directions:
a) Sauté the onions 8-10 minutes, stirring frequently; remove from heat and drain. Remove the casing from Braunschweiger and mix meat with the cream cheese until smooth. Mix in onions and pepper.
b) Serve as a liver spread on crackers, thinly sliced party rye or serve as a dip accompanied by a variety of fresh raw vegetables like carrots, celery, broccoli, radishes, cauliflower or cherry tomatoes.

62.   <u>Baked artichoke party dip</u>

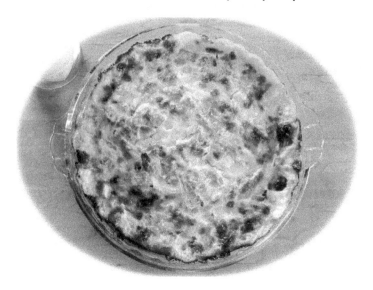

Ingredients:

- 1 Loaf large dark rye bread
- 2 tablespoons Butter
- 1 bunch Green onions; chopped
- 6 Cloves of fresh garlic; minced finely, up to 8
- 8 ounces Cream cheese; at room temp.
- 16 ounces Sour cream
- 12 ounces Shredded cheddar cheese
- 1 can (14 oz.) artichoke hearts; drained and cut into quarters (water packed not marinated)

Directions:

a) Cut a hole in the top of the bread loaf about 5 inches in diameter. Remove soft bread from cut portion and discard. Reserve crust to make top for loaf.

b) Scoop out most of the soft inside portion of the loaf and save for other purposes, such as stuffing or dried bread crumbs. In the butter,

c) Sauté the green onions and the garlic until the onions wilt. Cut the cream cheese into small chunks, add the onions, garlic, sour cream and cheddar cheese. Mix well. Fold in artichoke hearts, Out all of this mixture into hollowed out bread. Place top on bread and wrap in a heavy duty aluminium foil. Bake in 350 degree oven for $1\frac{1}{2}$ hours.

d) When ready, remove foil and serve, using cocktail rye bread to dip out the sauce.

63.   <u>Asparagus and feta canapés</u>

Ingredient
- 20 slices Thin white bread
- 4 ounces Blue cheese
- 8 ounces Cream cheese
- 1 Egg
- 20 Spears canned asparagus drained
- $\frac{1}{2}$ cup Melted butter

Directions:

a) Trim crusts from bread and flatten with a rolling pin. Blend cheeses and egg to a workable consistency and spread evenly on each slice of bread. Place an asparagus spear on each slice and roll up. Dip in melted butter to coat thoroughly. Place on cookie sheet and freeze.

b) When firmly frozen, slice into bite size pieces. (If freezing for a future date, place bite size pieces in a freezer bag - do not defrost to cook) Place on cookie sheet and bake at 400 F for 20 min.

64. Broiled seafood canapés

Ingredient
- 1 cup Cooked seafood, flaked
- 6 slices White bread
- $\frac{1}{4}$ cup Butter
- $\frac{1}{4}$ cup Cheddar or 1/3 cup ketchup or chili sauce
- American cheese, grated

Directions:
a) Toast bread on one side; trim off crusts and cut bread in half.
b) Butter untoasted sides; cover with a layer of seafood, then ketchup and top with cheese. Place canapés on a baking sheet under the broiler.
c) Broil until the cheese is melted and the canapés are heated through.
d) Makes 12 canapés.

65. <u>Caviar canapés and hors d'oeuvres</u>

Ingredient
- bread cut into shapes or Melbas
- egg salad spread
- a spread of caviar, minced onion and lemon
- juice
- a single small shrimp as a garnish.
- one ring of sliced, raw, mild onion

Directions:
a) dip slice of cucumber in French Dressing and place inside onion ring
b) cover cucumber with small mound of caviar seasoned with lemon and onion juice
c) Garnish with capers, chives or riced hard cooked eggs.

66. <u>Fromage-chevre canapés</u>

Ingredient
- 10 smalls Red potatoes, (3/4 pound)
- Vegetable cooking spray
- $\frac{1}{4}$ teaspoon Salt
- $\frac{1}{4}$ cup Skim milk
- 6 ounces Chevre, (mild goat cheese)
- 20 Belgian endive leaves, (3 medium head)
- 10 Seedless red grapes, halved
- 1 tablespoon Caviar

Directions:
a) Steam potatoes, covered, 13 minutes or until tender; let cool.
b) Lightly coat potatoes with cooking spray, and cut in half. Cut and discard a thin slice from the bottom of each potato half so they will stand up.
c) Sprinkle potato halves with salt.
d) Combine milk and cheese in a bowl; stir well.
e) Spoon mixture into a pastry bag fitted with a large star tip; pipe mixture onto potato halves and into endive leaves. Top each endive leaf with one grape half. Cover and chill, if desired.

67. Hearty mushroom canapés

Ingredient
- ¼ cup Chopped mushrooms
- ¼ cup Shredded Monterey Jack Cheese
- ¼ cup Mayonnaise
- 3 slices Rye bread
- 1½ teaspoon Grated Parmesan cheese

Directions:

a) Toast the rye bread and slice in half.
b) Cover each half with mushroom-cheese mixture and sprinkle with Parmesan and bake at 350 F. for 15-20 minutes or until cheese is bubbly.

68.   Rumaki canapés

Ingredient
- ½ cup Water
- 1 teaspoon Chicken bouillon
- 250 grams Chicken livers
- 1 tablespoon Shoyu
- ½ teaspoon Onion powder, dry mustard
- ¼ teaspoon Nutmeg
- ¼ cup Dry sherry
- 1 dash Pepper sauce
- 220 grams Water chestnuts
- 6 Bacon

Directions:

a) In 1-quart casserole, combine water, bouillon and livers. Cook on high 4-5 minutes until no longer pink. Drain.

b) Cook bacon on paper towel on high 5-6 minutes until crisp. Crumble and set aside.

c) Put livers, shoyu, onion and mustard, nutmeg and sherry into food processor. Blend until smooth. Add pepper sauce sparingly. Stir in water chestnuts and bacon.

d) Spread thickly on toast triangles or crackers. Prepare in advance and reheat by arranging on paper lined plate. Use med-high power 1-2 minutes until heated through.

e) Garnish with olive slice or pimento.

69. Salmon mousse canapés

Ingredient
- 7½ ounce Canned red salmon, drained
- 2 ounces Smoked salmon, cut in 1-inch pieces
- ¼ teaspoon Grated lemon rind
- 3 tablespoons Nonfat mayonnaise
- 1 tablespoon Fresh lemon juice
- ¼ cup Minced red bell pepper
- 2 tablespoons Minced green onions
- 1 tablespoon Minced fresh parsley
- 1 dash Freshly ground pepper
- 8 slices Party-style pumpernickel bread
- 8 slices Party-style rye bread
- 4 Rye crispbread crackers, broken in half
- ½ cup Alfalfa sprouts

Directions:

a) Discard skin and bones from canned salmon; flake salmon with a fork.

b) Position knife blade in food processor bowl; add salmon, smoked salmon, and next 3 ingredients. Process until smooth.

c) Pour into a bowl; stir in bell pepper and next 3 ingredients. Cover and chill. Yield: 2 dozen appetizers (serving size: 1 appetizer).

70.   <u>Sprouts-stuffed canapés</u>

Ingredient
- 1 pack canapés of desired shape
- 1 cup Bean sprouts
- $\frac{1}{2}$ cup Finely chopped onion
- $\frac{1}{2}$ cup Finely chopped tomato
- $\frac{1}{4}$ cup Finely chopped coriander
- $\frac{1}{4}$ cup Finely chopped boiled potato
- $\frac{1}{2}$ Lemon
- Salt to taste
- Freshly ground cumin seed powder
- 4 Green chillies finely chopped; (4 to 5)
- 1 cup Fine bikaneri sev; (optional)
- $\frac{1}{2}$ cup Tamarind chutney
- $\frac{1}{2}$ cup Green chutney
- Oil to deep fry or oven to bake

Directions:

a) Deep fry them till light brown. Drain on kitchen towel. Do all the canapés and keep them aside.

b) Mix the onion, tomato, potatoes, half the coriander, lemon, salt and green chilli together. Chill it for some time.

c) Before serving fill mixture in the canapés, put a dash of both chutneys on top. Sprinkle a pinch of salt and cumin powder (jeera). Garnish with sev and remaining coriander.

71. <u>Tuna and cucumber bites</u>

- 2 (5-ounce) cans tuna packed in water, drained
- 2 large hard-boiled eggs, peeled and chopped
- 1/2 cup mayonnaise
- 1/2 teaspoon salt
- 1/2 teaspoon black pepper
- 2 teaspoons goat cheese
- 1 medium cucumber, cut into rounds

Directions:

a) Put tuna in a medium bowl with chopped eggs, mayonnaise, salt, and pepper. Mash with a fork until combined.

b) Spread an equal amount of goat cheese on each cucumber slice and top with tuna salad mixture.

72.   <u>Beet appetizer salad</u>

Ingredient

- 2 pounds Beets
- Salt
- $\frac{1}{2}$ each Spanish onion, diced
- 4 Tomatoes, skinned, seeded and diced
- 2 tablespoons Vinegar
- 8 tablespoons Olive oil
- Black olives
- 2 each Garlic cloves, chopped
- 4 tablespoons Italian parsley, chopped
- 4 tablespoons Cilantro, chopped
- 4 mediums Potatoes, boiled
- Salt and pepper
- Hot red pepper

Directions:

a) Cut off ends of beets. Wash well and cook in boiling salted water until tender. Drain and remove skins under running cold water. Dice.

b) Mix together the dressing ingredients.

c) Combine beets in a salad bowl with the onion, tomato, garlic cilantro and parsley. Pour over half the dressing, toss gently and chill for 30 minutes. Slice the potatoes, place in a shallow bowl and toss with remaining dressing. Chill.

d) When ready to assemble, arrange beets, tomato and onion in the centre of a shallow bowl and arrange potatoes in a ring around them. Garnish with olives.

73.   <u>Curried egg salad endive cups</u>

Ingredient

- 1 large hard-boiled egg, peeled
- 1 teaspoon curry powder
- 1 tablespoon coconut oil
- $1/8$ teaspoon sea salt
- $1/8$ teaspoon black pepper
- 2 Belgian endive leaves, washed and dried

Directions:

A) IN A SMALL FOOD PROCESSOR, MIX ALL INGREDIENTS EXCEPT ENDIVE UNTIL WELL BLENDED.

B) SCOOP 1 TABLESPOON EGG SALAD MIXTURE ONTO EACH ENDIVE CUP.

C) SERVE IMMEDIATELY.

74.   Nasturtium shrimp appetizer salad

Ingredient

- 2 teaspoons Fresh lemon juice
- $\frac{1}{4}$ cup Olive oil
- Salt and pepper
- 1 cup Cooked shrimp; chopped
- 2 tablespoons Minced onion
- 1 small Tomato; cubed
- 1 Avocado; cubed
- Lettuce leaves
- 2 tablespoons Chopped nasturtium leaves
- Nasturtium flowers

Directions:

a) Whisk together the lemon juice and oil. Season with salt and pepper. Add the onion and shrimp and mix. Let stand 15 minutes.

b) Add the tomato, avocado and chopped nasturtium leaves. Mound on lettuce leaves and surround with fresh whole nasturtium flowers.

75. Zucchini appetizer salad

Ingredient

- ½ cup Fresh lemon juice
- ½ cup Salad oil
- 1 large Garlic clove
- Salt and pepper to taste
- 2 pinches Sugar
- 8 Zucchini
- Lettuce leaves
- 2 mediums Size tomatoes
- ½ small Green pepper chopped
- 3 tablespoons Very finely chopped scallion
- 1 tablespoon Capers
- 1 Sprig parsley
- 1 teaspoon Basil
- ½ teaspoon Oregano

Directions:

a) Dressing: Combine all the ingredients and set aside.

b) Salad: Simmer unpeeled whole zucchini in salted water for about 5 minutes uncovered. Pour off the hot water and rinse with cold water immediately to stop the cooking process. Drain. Cut each zucchini in half lengthwise.

c) Carefully scoop out the pulp. Lay zucchini, cut side up in a flat non metal dish. Cover with half the dressing.

d) Cover tightly with foil. place in refrigerator to marinate at least 4 hours.

76.   Pepper salad appetizer

Ingredient

77. 6 larges Sweet peppers
78. 1 medium Onion; coarsely chopped
79. Salt and pepper to taste
80. 3 tablespoons Vinegar (more if desired)
81. $\frac{1}{4}$ cup Olive oil
82. Oregano

Directions:

a) Bake peppers in hot 450 F oven for about 20 minutes or until wilted and soft. Remove seeds and outer skin.
b) Cut in pieces and place in a bowl. Add onion, salt and pepper. Mix vinegar and olive oil and add to peppers.
c) Sprinkle with oregano. Adjust seasoning if necessary.

77.   Party antipasto salad

Ingredient

- 1 can (16 oz.) artichoke hearts; drained/halved
- 1 pounds Frozen brussel sprouts
- $\frac{3}{4}$ pounds Cherry tomatoes
- 1 Jar (5 3/4 oz.) green Spanish olives; drained
- 1 Jar (12 oz.) pepperoncini peppers; drained
- 1 pounds Fresh mushrooms; cleaned
- 1 can (16 oz.) hearts of palm; optional
- 1 pounds Pepperoni or salami; cubed
- 1 Jar (16 oz.) black olives; drained
- $\frac{1}{4}$ cup Red wine vinegar
- $\frac{3}{4}$ cup Olive oil
- $\frac{1}{2}$ teaspoon Sugar
- 1 teaspoon Dijon mustard
- Salt; to taste
- Freshly ground pepper; to taste

Directions:

a) Combine all ingredients before adding the vinaigrette.
b) Refrigerate for 24 hours.

78. Pink party salad

Ingredient

- 1 can (No 2) crushed pineapple
- 24 larges Marshmallows
- 1 pack Strawberry Jello
- 1 cup Whipping cream
- 2 cups Sm. curd cottage cheese
- $\frac{1}{2}$ cup Nuts; chopped

Directions:

a) Heat juice from pineapple with marshmallows and Jello. Cool.

b) Mix whipped cream, pineapple, cottage cheese and nuts. Add first mixture and fold in.

c) Chill overnight.

79.   Cajun spam party salad

Ingredient

- 8 ounces Wagon wheel shape pasta
- 1 can Marinated artichoke hearts (6 oz)
- 1 can SPAM Luncheon Meat, cubed (12 oz)
- ⅓ cup Olive oil
- ¼ cup Creole seasoning mix
- 1 tablespoon Lemon juice
- 1 tablespoon Mayonnaise or salad dressing
- 1 tablespoon White wine vinegar
- 1 cup Diced bell pepper
- ½ cup Chopped red onion
- ½ cup Sliced ripe olives
- Fresh basil and Dried oregano
- ½ teaspoon Dry mustard
- ½ teaspoon Dried thyme leaves
- 1 Garlic clove, chopped

Directions:

a) Drain artichokes, reserving marinade; cut into quarters.

b) In large bowl, combine all salad ingredients. In blender, combine reserved artichoke marinade with remaining dressing ingredients.

c) Process until smooth. Add dressing to salad, tossing well. Cover and chill several hours or overnight.

80. Cocktail teriyaki

Ingredient

- 3½ pounds Lean beef
- 1 cup Soy sauce
- 3 Cloves garlic; finely minced
- 2 tablespoons Fresh grated ginger
- 1 teaspoon Accent

Directions:

a) Cut beef into ½-inch cubes. Combine soy sauce, ginger, garlic and Accent.

b) Let mixture blend for 1 hour. Add to beef and marinate overnight in refrigerator in a plastic bag or shallow covered plastic or glass container, stirring occasionally.

c) Skewer meat cubes on small bamboo sticks, about 4-5 per stick. Makes about 70 cocktail kabobs.

d) Arrange attractively on foil-covered tray and let guests broil individually on habachi or grill.

81. Prosciutto chips

Ingredient

- 12 (1-ounce) slices prosciutto

- Oil

Directions:

A) PREHEAT OVEN TO 350°F.

B) LINE A BAKING SHEET WITH PARCHMENT PAPER AND LAY PROSCIUTTO SLICES OUT IN A SINGLE LAYER. BAKE 12 MINUTES OR UNTIL PROSCIUTTO IS CRISPY.

C) LET COOL COMPLETELY BEFORE EATING.

82.   Beet chips

Ingredient

- 10 medium red beets
- 1/2 cup avocado oil
- 2 teaspoons sea salt
- 1/2 teaspoon granulated garlic

Directions:

A) PREHEAT OVEN TO 350°F. LINE A FEW BAKING SHEETS WITH PARCHMENT PAPER AND SET ASIDE.

B) PEEL BEETS WITH A VEGETABLE SLICER AND CUT OFF ENDS. CAREFULLY SLICE BEETS INTO ROUNDS, ABOUT 3 MM THICK, WITH A MANDOLINE SLICER OR A SHARP KNIFE.

C) PLACE SLICED BEETS IN A LARGE BOWL AND ADD OIL, SALT, AND GRANULATED GARLIC. TOSS TO COAT EACH SLICE. SET ASIDE 20 MINUTES, ALLOWING SALT TO PULL OUT EXCESS MOISTURE.

D) DRAIN EXCESS LIQUID AND ARRANGE SLICED BEETS IN A SINGLE LAYER ON PREPARED BAKING SHEETS. BAKE 45 MINUTES OR UNTIL CRISP.

E) REMOVE FROM OVEN AND ALLOW TO COOL. STORE IN AN AIRTIGHT CONTAINER UNTIL READY TO EAT, UP TO 1 WEEK.

83.   <u>Barley chips</u>

Ingredient

- 1 cup All-purpose flour
- $\frac{1}{2}$ cup Barley flour
- $\frac{1}{2}$ cup Rolled barley (barley
- Flakes)
- 2 tablespoons Sugar
- $\frac{1}{4}$ teaspoon Salt
- 8 tablespoons (1 stick) butter or
- Margarine, softened
- $\frac{1}{2}$ cup Milk

Directions:

a) In a large bowl or in the food processor, stir together the flours, barley, sugar, and salt.

b) Cut in the butter until the mixture resembles coarse meal. Add enough of the milk to form a dough that will hold together in a cohesive ball.

c) Divide the dough into 2 equal portions for rolling. On a floured surface or pastry cloth, roll out to $\frac{1}{8}$ to $\frac{1}{4}$ inch. Cut into 2-inch circles or squares and place on a lightly greased or parchment-lined baking sheet. Prick each cracker in 2 or 3 places with the tines of a fork.

d) Bake for 20 to 25 minutes, or until medium brown. Cool on a wire rack.

84. <u>Cheddar mexi-melt crisps</u>

Ingredient
- 1 cup shredded sharp Cheddar cheese
- $1/_8$ teaspoon granulated garlic
- $1/_8$ teaspoon chili powder
- $1/_8$ teaspoon ground cumin
- $1/_{16}$ teaspoon cayenne pepper
- 1 tablespoon finely chopped cilantro
- 1 teaspoon olive oil

Directions:

A) PREHEAT OVEN TO 350°F. PREPARE A COOKIE SHEET WITH PARCHMENT PAPER OR A SILPAT MAT.

B) MIX ALL INGREDIENTS IN A MEDIUM BOWL UNTIL WELL COMBINED.

C) DROP BY TABLESPOON-SIZED PORTIONS ONTO PREPARED COOKIE SHEET.

D) COOK 5-7 MINUTES UNTIL EDGES BEGIN TO BROWN.

E) ALLOW TO COOL 2-3 MINUTES BEFORE REMOVING FROM COOKIE SHEET WITH A SPATULA.

85.   <u>Pepperoni chips</u>

Ingredient

- 24 slices sugar-free pepperoni

- Oil

Directions:

A) PREHEAT OVEN TO 425°F.

B) LINE A BAKING SHEET WITH PARCHMENT PAPER AND LAY OUT PEPPERONI SLICES IN A SINGLE LAYER.

C) BAKE 10 MINUTES AND THEN REMOVE FROM OVEN AND USE A PAPER TOWEL TO BLOT AWAY EXCESS GREASE. RETURN TO THE OVEN 5 MORE MINUTES OR UNTIL PEPPERONI IS CRISPY.

86.   Angel crisps

Ingredient

- ½ cup Sugar
- ½ cup Brown sugar
- 1 cup Shortening
- 1 Egg
- 1 teaspoon Vanilla
- 1 teaspoon Cream of tartar
- 2 cups Flour
- ½ teaspoon Salt
- 1 teaspoon Baking soda

Directions:

a) Cream sugar, brown sugar and shortening. Add vanilla and egg. Blend until fluffy. Add the dry ingredients; blend.

b) Roll teaspoonfuls into balls. Dip into water and then into granulated sugar. Lay on cookie sheet, sugar side up, then flatten with a glass.

c) Bake at 350 degrees for 10 minutes.

87. <u>Chicken skin crisps satay</u>

Ingredient

- Skin from 3 large chicken thighs
- 2 tablespoons no-sugar-added chunky peanut butter
- 1 tablespoon unsweetened coconut cream
- 1 teaspoon coconut oil
- 1 teaspoon seeded and minced jalapeño pepper
- 1/4 clove garlic, minced
- 1 teaspoon coconut aminos

Directions:

A) PREHEAT OVEN TO 350°F. ON A COOKIE SHEET LINED WITH PARCHMENT PAPER, LAY OUT SKINS AS FLAT AS POSSIBLE.

B) BAKE 12–15 MINUTES UNTIL SKINS TURN LIGHT BROWN AND CRISPY, BEING CAREFUL NOT TO BURN THEM.

C) REMOVE SKINS FROM COOKIE SHEET AND PLACE ON A PAPER TOWEL TO COOL.

D) IN A SMALL FOOD PROCESSOR, ADD PEANUT BUTTER, COCONUT CREAM, COCONUT OIL, JALAPEÑO, GARLIC, AND COCONUT AMINOS. MIX UNTIL WELL BLENDED, ABOUT 30 SECONDS.

E) CUT EACH CRISPY CHICKEN SKIN IN 2 PIECES.

F) PLACE 1 TABLESPOON PEANUT SAUCE ON EACH CHICKEN CRISP AND SERVE IMMEDIATELY. IF SAUCE IS TOO RUNNY, REFRIGERATE 2 HOURS BEFORE USING.

88. Chicken skin with avocado

Ingredient

- Skin from 3 large chicken thighs
- 1/4 medium avocado, peeled and pitted
- 3 tablespoons full-fat sour cream
- 1/2 medium jalapeño pepper, seeded and finely chopped
- 1/2 teaspoon sea salt

Directions:

A) PREHEAT OVEN TO 350°F. ON A COOKIE SHEET LINED WITH PARCHMENT PAPER LAY OUT SKINS AS FLAT AS POSSIBLE.

B) BAKE 12-15 MINUTES UNTIL SKINS TURN LIGHT BROWN AND CRISPY, BEING CAREFUL NOT TO BURN THEM.

C) REMOVE SKINS FROM COOKIE SHEET AND PLACE ON A PAPER TOWEL TO COOL.

D) IN A SMALL BOWL, COMBINE AVOCADO, SOUR CREAM, JALAPEÑO, AND SALT.

E) MIX WITH A FORK UNTIL WELL BLENDED.

F) CUT EACH CRISPY CHICKEN SKIN IN 2 PIECES.

G) PLACE 1 TABLESPOON AVOCADO MIX ON EACH CHICKEN CRISP AND SERVE IMMEDIATELY.

89. Parmesan vegetable crisps

Ingredient

- 3/4 cup shredded zucchini
- 1/4 cup shredded carrots
- 2 cups freshly shredded Parmesan cheese
- 1 tablespoon olive oil
- 1/4 teaspoon black pepper

Directions:

A) PREHEAT OVEN TO 375°F. PREPARE A COOKIE SHEET WITH PARCHMENT PAPER OR A SILPAT MAT.

B) WRAP SHREDDED VEGETABLES IN A PAPER TOWEL AND WRING OUT EXCESS MOISTURE.

C) MIX ALL INGREDIENTS IN A MEDIUM BOWL UNTIL THOROUGHLY COMBINED.

D) PLACE TABLESPOON-SIZED MOUNDS ONTO PREPARED COOKIE SHEET.

E) BAKE 7-10 MINUTES UNTIL LIGHTLY BROWNED.

F) LET COOL 2-3 MINUTES AND REMOVE FROM COOKIE SHEET.

90.   Pumpkin pie coconut crisps

Ingredient

- 2 tablespoons coconut oil
- 1/₂ teaspoon vanilla extract
- 1/₂ teaspoon pumpkin pie spice
- 1 tablespoon granulated erythritol
- 2 cups unsweetened coconut flakes
- 1/₈ teaspoon salt

Directions:

A) PREHEAT OVEN TO 350°F.

B) PUT COCONUT OIL IN A MEDIUM MICROWAVE-SAFE BOWL AND MICROWAVE UNTIL MELTED, ABOUT 20 SECONDS. ADD VANILLA EXTRACT, PUMPKIN PIE SPICE, AND GRANULATED ERYTHRITOL TO COCONUT OIL AND STIR UNTIL COMBINED.

C) PLACE COCONUT FLAKES IN A MEDIUM BOWL, POUR COCONUT OIL MIXTURE OVER THEM, AND TOSS TO COAT. SPREAD OUT IN A SINGLE LAYER ON A COOKIE SHEET AND SPRINKLE WITH SALT.

D) BAKE 5 MINUTES OR UNTIL COCONUT IS CRISPY.

91.   <u>Chicken skin crisps alfredo</u>

Ingredient

- Skin from 3 large chicken thighs
- 2 tablespoons ricotta cheese
- 2 tablespoons cream cheese
- 1 tablespoon grated Parmesan cheese
- 1/4 clove garlic, minced
- 1/4 teaspoon ground white pepper

Directions:

a) Preheat oven to 350°F. On a cookie sheet lined with parchment paper, lay out skins as flat as possible.

b) Bake 12-15 minutes until skins turn light brown and crispy, being careful not to burn them.

c) Remove skins from cookie sheet and place on a paper towel to cool.

d) In a small bowl, add cheeses, garlic, and pepper. Mix with a fork until well blended.

e) Cut each crispy chicken skin in 2 pieces.

f) Place 1 tablespoon cheese mix on each chicken crisp and serve immediately.

92. Apple and Peanut Butter Stackers

Ingredients
- 2 medium apples
- 1/3 cup chunky peanut butter
- Optional fillings: granola, miniature semisweet chocolate chips

Directions
a) Core apples. Cut each apple crosswise into six slices. Spread peanut butter over six slices; sprinkle with fillings of your choice.
b) Top with remaining apple slices.

93.   <u>Fried Green Tomatoes</u>

Ingredients

- 1/4 cup fat-free mayonnaise
- 1/4 teaspoon grated lime zest
- 2 tablespoons lime juice
- 1 teaspoon minced fresh thyme or 1/4 teaspoon dried thyme
- 1/2 teaspoon pepper, divided
- 1/4 cup all-purpose flour
- 2 large egg whites, lightly beaten
- 3/4 cup cornmeal
- 1/4 teaspoon salt
- 2 medium green tomatoes
- 2 medium red tomatoes
- 2 tablespoons canola oil
- 8 slices Canadian bacon

Directions

a) Mix the first 4 ingredients and 1/4 teaspoon pepper; refrigerate until serving. Place flour in a shallow bowl; place egg whites in a separate shallow bowl. In a third bowl, mix cornmeal, salt and remaining pepper.

b) Cut each tomato crosswise into 4 slices. Dredge 1 slice in flour to lightly coat; shake off excess. Dip in egg whites, then in cornmeal mixture. Repeat with remaining tomato slices.

c) In a large nonstick skillet, heat oil over medium heat. In batches, cook tomatoes until golden brown, 4-5 minutes per side.

d) In same pan, lightly brown Canadian bacon on both sides. For each, stack 1 slice each green tomato, bacon and red tomato. Serve with sauce.

94.   <u>The No-Bread BLT</u>

yield: 1 SERVING

Ingredients

- 6 slices bacon, cut in half horizontally
- lettuce leaves
- fresh tomato, sliced

Directions

a) Place three slices next to each other in a vertical row on a baking tray lined with a silicone mat.

b) Flap the top of the outer two slices down, then place a slice of bacon horizontally across them.

c) Flap the bacon back up, then flap up the central slice, and place another horizontal slice in the middle. Then add the final horizontal slice at the bottom by flapping up the two outer slices.

d) Repeat to form another bacon weave (you will need two per BLT).

e) Place an inverted non-stick rack over the top of the bacon and cook under a preheated broiler until the bacon starts to go crispy. Remove the rack, and flip over the bacon. Return to the broiler if necessary.

f) Transfer the bacon weaves to kitchen paper to drain the excess fat.

g) Add sliced tomato and crunchy romaine lettuce to one bacon weave, then top with the second weave.

95. Apple, Ham, and Cheese Sandwiches

Servings: 2

Ingredients

- apple
- Ham slices
- Colby Jack Slices
- Brown Mustard, Dijon style or condiment of choice

Directions

a) Slice apples into rings.

b) Add Ham slices. Top with cheese slices.

c) Spread mustard on the top ring of the sandwich and place on top (condiment side down).

96. <u>Sweet Potato Burger Buns</u>

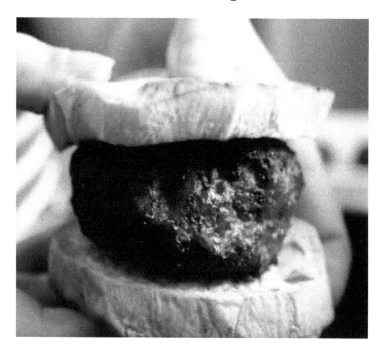

Ingredients

- 1 Large Sweet Potato
- 2 Teaspoons Olive Oil
- Salt and Pepper

Directions

a) Peel and dice your sweet potatoes into the shapes of burger buns.

b) You need 2 medium slices for each burger you are making. You can cook up to 16 slices at once in the air fryer, before your air fryer becomes overcrowded.

c) Using your hands rub the olive oil over them.

d) Season with salt and pepper.

e) Cook for 10 minutes at 180c/360f in the air fryer.

f) Place your Mediterranean burgers in between two sweet potato burger bun slices and serve.

97. <u>Cucumber Subs</u>

SERVES 2

Ingredients

- 2 cucumbers
- deli meat-turkey, ham, or other deli meat slices or shaved
- bacon (optional)
- green onions (optional)
- tomatoes (optional)
- any sandwich fillers (optional)
- laughing cow cheese or mayo or cream cheese or any other condiment

Directions

a) Cut the cucumber length-wise, from tip to tip. Scoop out the inside of the cucumber to make room for your sandwich fillers. Add meat, veggies, and other sandwich makings to the inside of the cucumber.

b) Place one half of the cucumber on the other half. Enjoy!!

98.   <u>Breadless Italian Sub Sandwich</u>

Yield: 4 sandwiches

Ingredients

- 8 large Portobello mushrooms, wiped clean
- 2 tablespoons extra-virgin olive oil
- Kosher salt
- 1 tablespoon red wine vinegar
- 1 tablespoon finely chopped pepperoncini with seeds
- 1/2 teaspoon dried oregano
- Freshly ground black pepper
- 2 ounces sliced provolone (about 4 slices)
- 2 ounces thinly sliced low-sodium ham (about 4 slices)
- 1 ounce thinly sliced Genoa salami (about 4 slices)
- 1 small tomato, cut into 4 slices
- 1/2 cup shredded iceberg lettuce
- 4 pimento-stuffed olives

Directions

a) Position an oven rack in the top third of the oven and preheat the oven broiler.

b) Remove the stems from the mushrooms and discard. Lay the mushroom caps gill-side-up and use a sharp knife to completely remove the gills (so that the caps will lie flat). Arrange the mushroom caps on a baking sheet, brush all over with 1 tablespoon of oil and sprinkle with 1/4 teaspoon salt. Broil until the caps are just tender, flipping halfway through, 4 to 5 minutes per side. Allow to cool completely.

c) Whisk together the vinegar, pepperoncini, oregano, remaining 1 tablespoon oil and a few grinds of black pepper in a small bowl.

d) Assemble the sandwiches: Arrange one mushroom cap, cut side-up, on a work surface. Fold 1 piece of provolone to fit on top of the cap and repeat with 1 slice each of ham and salami.

e) Top with 1 slice of tomato and about 2 tablespoons of lettuce. Drizzle with some of the pepperoncini vinaigrette. Sandwich with another mushroom cap and secure with a toothpick threaded with an olive. Repeat with the remaining ingredients to make 3 more sandwiches.

f) Wrap each sandwich halfway in wax paper (this will help catch all the juices) and serve.

99. <u>Mac and Cheese Slider</u>

Serving Size: 12

Ingredients:
- 1 Cup Macaroni pasta
- 1 tablespoon butter
- Pepper to taste
- 1 $\frac{1}{2}$ teaspoons all-purpose flour
- $\frac{1}{2}$ cup milk
- $\frac{3}{4}$ cup cheddar cheese, shredded
- 18 oz. Hawaiian sweet rolls
- 16 oz. barbecue shredded pork, cooked
- 1 tablespoon honey
- $\frac{1}{2}$ teaspoon ground mustard
- 2 tablespoons butter, melted

Directions
a) Preheat your oven to 375 degrees F.
b) Cook the pasta according to the directions in the package.
c) Drain and set aside.
d) Add the butter to a pan over medium heat.
e) Stir in the pepper and flour.
f) Stir until smooth.
g) Bring to a boil, stirring.
h) Cook for 3 to 5 minutes.
i) Add the cheese and cook while stirring until melted.
j) Add the cooked pasta to the pan.
k) Arrange the roll bottoms in a baking pan.
l) Top with the cheese and pasta mixture, shredded pork, and roll tops.

m) In a small bowl, mix the honey, mustard and butter.
n) Brush tops with this mixture.
o) Bake in the oven for 10 minutes.

100. Turkey Sliders with Sweet Potato

Makes 10 servings

Ingredients
- 4 Applewood-smoked bacon strips, finely chopped
- 1-pound ground turkey
- 1/2 cup panko crumbs
- 2 large eggs
- 1/2 cup grated Parmesan cheese
- 4 tablespoons chopped fresh cilantro
- 1 teaspoon dried basil
- 1/2 teaspoon ground cumin
- 1 tablespoon soy sauce
- 2 large sweet potatoes
- Shredded Colby-Monterey Jack cheese

Directions
a) In a large skillet, cook bacon over medium heat until crisp; drain on paper towels. Discard all but 2 tablespoons drippings. Set skillet aside. Combine bacon with next 8 ingredients until well mixed; cover and refrigerate at least 30 minutes.
b) Preheat oven to 425°. Cut sweet potatoes into 20 slices about 1/2 in. thick. Place slices on an ungreased baking sheet; bake until sweet potatoes are tender but not mushy, 30-35 minutes. Remove slices; cool on a wire rack.
c) Heat skillet with reserved drippings over medium-high heat. Shape turkey mixture into slider-sized patties. Cook sliders in batches, 3-4 minutes on each side, taking care not to crowd skillet. Add a pinch of shredded cheddar after flipping each slider the first

time. Cook until a thermometer reads 165° and juices run clear.

d) To serve, place each slider on a sweet potato slice; dab with honey Dijon mustard. Cover with a second sweet potato slice. Pierce with toothpick.

CONCLUSION

Tailgating is an excellent opportunity to enjoy delicious food and drinks while spending time with loved ones before a sporting event. Whether you're grilling up burgers and hot dogs or serving up savory dips and snacks, tailgating recipes are sure to satisfy any appetite. So fire up the grill, grab your friends and family, and get ready for a fun-filled day of sports and great food. With these easy-to-make tailgating recipes, you'll be sure to have a winning game day.

Ingram Content Group UK Ltd.
Milton Keynes UK
UKHW020721090623
423160UK00006B/17